# OSAMA BIN LADEN

# 100 THINGS YOU DIDN'T KNOW

By J. Adams

# TABLE OF CONTENTS

# INTRODUCTION

On September 11, 2001, millions of people around the world were shocked when they turned on their television sets and watched as two planes crashed into New York City's World Trade Center (the Twin Towers); another plane headed to Washington D.C. and crashed into a section of the Pentagon; and yet another plane crashed into a Pennsylvania field.

What people remember about that day is the vast number of lives that were lost. In the crashes at the Pentagon and Twin Towers alone, more than 3,000 people (inclusive of firefighters and police officers) lost their lives. People also remember the leader of al-Qaeda, the extremist Islamic group, taking responsibility for this vicious attack on the United States of America. The name of that leader was Osama bin Laden.

Much to the anguish and revulsion of most Americans and many others worldwide, from that day on, the world's most wanted man became a household name. Whether you were a five-year-old boy living in the United States whose firefighter father died that day, or you were an 85-year-old woman sitting in her rocking chair watching the news in London, you knew who Osama bin Laden was.

Contrary to what bin Laden's goal must have been for attacking the Twin Towers, the indomitable spirit of New Yorkers was not broken by the tragedy. There was fear, pain, anger and mourning, all of which gave way to resilience, defiance and pride – and a tribute to the Twin Towers and all who lost their lives to terrorism that day has risen up even higher into the sky. A 408-foot spire – which will serve as a world-class broadcast antenna – now makes One World Trade Center the tallest building in the United States.[1]

While talk of this man's life and atrocious acts was always buzzing through the air, there's a lot about him that the world doesn't know. Take a moment to journey into the life of this notorious fugitive, and find out 100 things that you probably didn't know about Osama bin Laden.

## EARLY LIFE & EDUCATION

Two areas of the life of Osama bin Laden that most people know little about are his youth and his education. Even though bin Laden was a member of a very large family, he was a privileged child and was also highly educated.

The following are 18 things that you probably didn't know about the early life and education of the world's most notorious terrorist:

1. Osama bin Laden was born on March 10, 1957, in Riyadh, Saudi Arabia. Of 50 children born to his father, bin Laden was the 7th-born. However, he was the only child from the union of his father and mother.

2. Bin Laden's father, Mohammed bin Awad bin Laden, was originally from the southern Yemen coast of Hadhramaut, and migrated to Saudi Arabia shortly before World War I. His mother (his father's 10th wife) was a Syrian named

Alia Ghanem, who later changed her name to Hamida al-Attas.

3. To most of the world, he was known as Osama bin Laden; however, his actual name is Osama bin Mohammed bin Awad bin Laden.

4. Bin Laden's name is of Arabic origin and means, "*Osama, son of Mohammed, son of Awad, son of Laden.*"

5. Bin Laden is not the family's surname. According to bin Laden's son, Omar bin Laden, the hereditary surname of the family is "*al-Qahtani.*" However, it is believed that Mohammed bin Laden never registered that name to be used by the family.  It is interesting, the way the name al-Qahtani turns up during bin inglorious terrorist career.  There was a certain female CIA agent whose role in the long hunt for bin Laden you can learn a bit about in the movie *Zero Dark Thirty.* During the search, this woman (who went by the alias "Maya") found a clue from information revealed during

the CIA torture/interrogation of one
Mohammed al-Qahtani.[2]

6. There are variations of the name Osama
   bin Laden. These include: Usama bin
   Laden, Oussama ben Laden and
   Ussamah bin Laden. The press also
   refers to him as OBL, or UBL.

7. Bin Laden's followers greatly respected
   him. One way they showed their respect
   was to refer to him by names that
   identified him as their leader. These
   names included: *Lion Sheik*; *Lion*; *the
   Director*; *Hajj*; *the Sheik al-Mujahid* or
   *Jihadist Sheik*; *the Sheik*; and *Emir or
   the Prince*.

8. Bin Laden came from a very large
   family. His father had a total of 22 wives,
   though supposedly never more than four
   at a time, as he continually divorced
   older wives and replaced them with
   new, younger wives.[3]  He had more than
   50 children, with Osama being his 17th
   child.

9. Bin Laden was the only child from the union of his mother and father. His parents divorced shortly after he was born, and his mother remarried. She took him to live with her new husband, with whom she had four more children. Bin Laden lived with his mother, stepfather and stepsiblings for most of his childhood.[4]

10. Bin Laden's father, Mohammed bin Awad bin Laden, started out as a poor laborer. He later founded his own construction company, the Saudi bin Laden Group. He was an astute businessman and eventually became a billionaire by transforming his company into the most successful construction company in the Saudi Kingdom. He gained favor with the Saudi royal family. Most of his business came from contracts with the Saudi royal family. Among major jobs the Saudi bin Laden Group did for the Kingdom was to design and build the al-Hada road, providing easier access for Muslims making the pilgrimage to Mecca in

Saudi Arabia; and rebuilding the mosques in the holy cities of Mecca and Medina. The bin Ladens became one of the wealthiest non-royal families in the Kingdom. Amid such wealth, bin Laden and his siblings grew up in very lavish surroundings. Bin Laden's father gained favor with the community at large for paying civil servants' salaries during a period when the city was unable to do so. [5]

11. Bin Laden's father was very strict, particularly towards his sons. He insisted that all his children practice a strict moral and religious code, and live under the same roof. However, after his parents divorced, bin Laden went to live with his mother and her new husband.

12. When bin Laden was 10 years old, his father died in a plane crash (September 3, 1967) while landing in southwest Saudi Arabia. This was reportedly due to the American pilot misjudging the landing.[6] At the time, bin Laden's father was on his way to the south of Saudi

Arabia to supervise a project his company was contracting.[7]

13. Bin Laden grew up during the 1960's and 70's, while there was much turmoil in the Middle East. He was first introduced to the Muslim Brotherhood (which was founded in the late 1920's in Egypt) at the age of 14. He adopted the Muslim Brotherhood at secondary school and at university, as many educated Muslims were inclined to do at the time.[8] His Muslim Brotherhood teachers exposed him to their ideas. As bin Laden got older, he started to break away from the Brotherhood. He openly criticized the members, accusing them of being disloyal to the jihad. The reasons for bin Laden's eventual religious extremism are unknown.

14. To many, bin Laden seemed to be a very somber person who didn't participate in fun activities. You'd be surprised to know, however, that during his early years, he enjoyed watching the

TV shows *Fury* and *Bonanza*. His youth was lived in great privilege. He was surrounded by servants and enjoyed the comfort of air-conditioned houses. Some university classmates remember him frequenting nightclubs, drinking and partying. However, we certainly know that he soon got fanatically serious about his religion and politics.[9]

15. Bin Laden was extremely dedicated to the jihad from a very young age. As a teenager, he formed a singing group (something like a glee club) so that he and his friends could sing songs about jihad.

16. Bin Laden was raised as a devout Wahhabi Muslim. Wahhabis are very conservative Sunni Muslims who want to eliminate all foreign influence in Islam. Additionally, they oppose Shiite Islam and Sufism (Islamic mysticism).

17. Bin Laden attended primary, secondary and tertiary institutions in Jeddah. He graduated from the King Abdul Aziz

University in 1979. Some say he had a degree in civil engineering, while others say that his degree was in public administration. In any case, it was at the university that he was introduced to the religious/political teachings of Sheik Abdullah Azzam, who advocated liberating Islamic nations from foreign influence.

"Bin Laden's mentor Abdullah Azzam frequently travels all over the world with the apparent support of the CIA. Slate will later write, "Azzam trotted the globe during the 1980s to promote the Afghan jihad against the Soviets. By the time of his death in 1989, he had recruited between 16,000 and 20,000 mujaheddin from 20 countries to Afghanistan, visited 50 American cities to advance his cause, and dispatched acolytes to spread the gospel in 26 US states, not to mention across the Middle East and Europe." Slate calls him "the Lenin of international jihad," noting that he "didn't invent his movement's ideas, but he furthered them and put them into practice around the world."[10] *[Slate, 4/16/2002]*

Sadly, all that recruiting helped build the strength of al-Qaeda and the jihad against the United States.

18. Although his primary interest was religion, bin Laden was also an avid reader. It is said that his favorite books included the works of Charles de Gaulle and Field Marshal Bernard Montgomery.

## MARRIAGES & CHILDREN

Osama bin Laden was known to be a very dedicated family man. He even showed support for family members that didn't share his beliefs.

Listed below are seven facts about his family life that most people didn't know:

19. In 1974, at the age of 17, bin Laden was married for the first time to his Syrian cousin Najwa. It is believed that the two separated shortly before the 9/11 attack on the United States.

   Bin Laden and Najwa had 11 children together. She left him before the 9/11 attacks. She supposedly admitted not being joyous about sharing her husband with other wives. Though they separated, they never divorced. Their son, Omar, explained that there is much prestige in being the first wife and cousin and the mother of the first son, and that it is rare for a Muslim man to divorce such a wife.[11]

20. After his first marriage, bin Laden was married five more times:

- o He married Khadijah in 1983. They divorced in 1995.

- o He married Khairiah in 1985. They were married until the time of his death in 2011.

- o Shiam became his fourth wife in 1987. They were also married until the time of his death.

- o In 1996, bin Laden married an unnamed woman; however, the marriage was annulled a few days after the ceremony.

- o He married his sixth wife, Amal, in 2001. This marriage also lasted until the time of his death.

21. Bin Laden had approximately 24 children.

- o 11 Children from his First Marriage – Abdullah (b. 1976), Abdul Rahman (b. 1978), Sa'ad (b. 1979), Omar (b. 1981), Osman (b. 1983), Muhammad (b. 1985), Fatima (b. 1987), Iman (b. 1990), Ladin "*Bakir*" (b. 1993), Rukhaiya (b. 1997) and Nour (b. 1999 or 2000).

- o Three Children from his Second Marriage – Ali (b. 1984 or 1986), Amer (b. 1990) and Aisha (b.1992).

- o One Child from his Third Marriage – Hamza (b. 1989 or 1991). It is believed that Hamza died during the raid on his father's Abbottabad compound.

- o Four Children from his Fourth Marriage – Kadhija (b. 1988),

Khalid (b. 1989), Miriam (b. 1990) and Sumaiya (b. 1992).

- o Five Children from his Sixth Marriage – Safiyah (b. 2001), Aasia (b. 2003), Ibrahim (b. 2005), Zainab (b. 2006) and Hussain (b. 2008).

22. One of bin Laden's sons, Abdul Rahman, was born with hydrocephalus (commonly known as "water on the brain"). It is believed that bin Laden traveled to London to seek medical advice about his son's condition. He returned to Saudi Arabia having decided against the suggested surgery. Bin Laden treated Abdul Rahman with a folk remedy; the child ultimately became mildly retarded.[12]

23. After news media exposed bin Laden's involvement in terror attacks around the world, a number of his family members disowned him. They were worried that the family's name was being taken over; they had severed ties with him after

failing to convince him to tone down his views.[13] However, his siblings still gave him his inheritance, as they believed that it was wrong to keep things (money, property, etc.) that didn't belong to them.

24. After the 9/11 attacks on the United States, a number of bin Laden's children fled to Iran. The Iranian government still closely monitors the movements of all his children living in the country. Bin Laden's actions made innocent victims of his children and grandchildren who may always be at risk of manifestations of fear and hatred simply because of their blood tie to such a notorious man.[14]

25. Bin Laden's first wife, Najwa, and their son, Omar, wrote about their lives as part of the bin Laden family. The book is entitled, "*Growing up bin Laden: Osama's Wife and Son Take Us Inside Their Secret World*." The book was published in October of 2009.

## FINANCES

Because of the simplicity of his appearance and lifestyle, there were quite a number of people who didn't know that Osama bin Laden was a very wealthy man. Those who knew him will tell you that rather than spending money on himself, he preferred using it to fund al-Qaeda and the jihad.

The following six facts that you probably didn't know about his finances:

26. Bin Laden's personal fortune was estimated to be more than $300 million. The majority of his fortune was the inheritance he received from his father's estate; the rest, he made on his own.

27. Following in his father's footsteps, bin Laden started a very successful construction company in Sudan, in addition to several other legitimate businesses across the Middle East and sections of North Africa. These businesses were in the sectors of

investment banking, agriculture and shipping.

28. Bin Laden invested a lot of his personal money in Sudan. He did this in order to obtain protection from the Sudanese government. Some of his investments included bakeries, roads, and his construction company. It is estimated that his investments in the country amounted to U.S. $200 million.

29. Because of the Sudanese government's weak financial status, they were unable to pay bin Laden for most his construction projects. He earned less than 10% from these projects; as a result, he lost a lot of money.

30. Despite his wealth, Osama bin Laden was known to live a very simple life. He advised his family to dress and eat simply as well. He thought that it was more important to spend money on the jihad than on worldly possessions.

31. Sidi Tayyib al-Madani, a former close aid of Osama bin Laden, eventually defected to the Saudi government. Al-Madani possessed many of bin Laden's financial records, which he gave to the Saudis. Bin Laden was aware of al-Madani's plans and was forced to liquidate as many of his businesses as possible, in order to prevent the Saudi government from repossessing them.

## APPEARANCE AND PERSONAL LIFE

Osama bin Laden was widely known as "*Public Enemy #1*." There are, however, quite a few details about his personal life that would interest many people.

Following are 17 of those interesting details that you probably didn't know:

32. Many pictures and videos of bin Laden showed him sitting down. Because of this, some people didn't have a clue as to how tall he was. According to information from the FBI, bin Laden's height was between 6'4" and 6'6".

33. Information released by the FBI states that bin Laden was left-handed.[15] Additionally, videos and pictures of him showed that he used his left hand to walk with his cane. On the other hand, however, there are videos and pictures showing him holding his cane with his right hand, and writing on paper with his

right hand.[16] Perhaps he was ambidextrous?

34. Bin Laden enjoyed writing poetry. When the Afghanistan al-Qaeda headquarters were raided in 2001, among the 1,500 audiocassettes that were found was some of bin Laden's poetry. Professor Flagg Miller described bin Laden "the poet" as being, "...*a skilled poet with clever rhymes and meters.*" According to the L.A. Times in September of 2008[17], following is a sample poem (or possibly an excerpt from a poem) by Osama bin Laden:

> A youth, who plunges into the smoke of war, smiling
> He hunches forth, staining the blades of lances red
> May God not let my eye stray from the most eminent
> Humans, should they fall, Djinn, should they ride
> [And] lions of the jungle, whose only fangs
> [Are their] lances and short Indian swords

As the stallion bears my witness
that I hold them back
[My] stabbing is like the cinders
of fire that explode into flame
On the day of the stallions'
expulsion, how the war-cries attest to
me
As do stabbing, striking, pens,
and books.

35. Although bin Laden was a native of
Saudi Arabia, he had stopped wearing
the traditional headdress for Saudi
males (the keffiyeh, which is a squared
cloth with a checkered pattern), opting
instead for a white turban. Bin Laden
stopped wearing the keffiyeh around the
time he became anti-Saudi.

36. One of the methods bin Laden used to
avoid detection was having his beard
shaved. Once his beard was shaved, he
became virtually unrecognizable, even
to those who knew him fairly well.

37. A year following the 9/11 attacks on the
United States, a limousine in which bin

Laden was traveling was pulled over due to speeding. The police officer looked inside the vehicle, didn't recognize anyone, and let them go with a simple warning. Bin Laden was unrecognizable because he had shaved his trademark beard.

38. During the war between the Soviet Union and Afghanistan, bin Laden left Saudi Arabia to fight in the war. He lost two of his toes while fighting. It is believed that this was one of the reasons he walked with a cane.

39. It is also thought that bin Laden walked with a cane because he suffered from kidney disease. Because of his illness, he required regular dialysis treatments.

40. Once, he was almost the victim of a chemical weapons attack. Luckily enough (for him at least), he was able to escape before suffering any damage.

41. Bombs often exploded in close proximity to bin Laden. As a result, there were a

few times when he required hospital
treatments for bodily injuries.

42. Bin Laden was aware of the fact that
American Special Forces were trying to
spy on him via satellite. Believe it or not,
he regularly wore a cowboy hat in order
to avoid satellite detection, and also
detection from people on the streets.

43. While one of his wives (Amal) was
pregnant, he took her to private clinics;
however, he made her pretend to be a
deaf mute so that she wouldn't be
questioned.

44. The French show, *Les Guignols de
l'info*, features a puppet that looks like
bin Laden. *Les Guignols de l'info* is a
satirical puppet show that mocks French
politicians and international newsmakers
as well.

45. Bin Laden was known to cook for and
serve his comrades from time to time.
Although he did this, he barely ate
anything himself. He chose to eat

morsels of food left on the plates of his guests or comrades, as he believed that by doing this, he would gain Allah's favor.

46. Bin Laden loved traveling, and had been to countries such as Sudan, Afghanistan, Pakistan, Syria and countries of the Arabian Peninsula. It is also believed that he traveled to Sweden with his siblings when he was younger.

47. Bin Laden was an avid fan of football (the sport Americans call soccer), and was a great supporter of the Arsenal Football Club. He also played football; his position was center forward.

48. Bin Laden was very fond of research, information gathering and media monitoring. A data management team always traveled with him, as a means of keeping him updated on what was happening across the world.

## IDEOLOGY & BELIEFS

Like the rest of us, Osama bin Laden lived by his beliefs. As we have come to learn, many of his beliefs were perverted from the norm - even the norm that was his religion.

Following are five things you probably didn't know about bin Laden's ideology and beliefs:

49. Bin Laden prohibited any type of electronic device from being close to him, as he believed that electronic devices could be monitored and would aid in targeting him. On the other hand, he liked to be kept up-to-date with the latest news.

50. Based on a special Islamic code that he followed from childhood and throughout his life, bin Laden didn't believe in investing his money in non-Islamic countries. He was a firm believer in not supporting anything that was anti-Islamic.

51. Bin Laden also didn't believe in the stock market or banks. He believed that both were controlled by the Jews and the Americans. He claimed that the policy of al-Qaeda was to *"bleed America to the point of bankruptcy."*

52. Bin Laden was anti-Semitic (meaning he discriminated against Jews). In 1998, during an al-Jazeera Arab television interview, he said, *"Every Muslim, the minute he can start differentiating, carries hate towards Americans, Jews and Christians."* Also in 1998, bin Laden joined forces with extremist groups from Bangladesh, Pakistan and Egypt, and created the *"International Islamic Front for Jihad Against the Jews and Crusaders."*

53. Bin Laden believed that legitimate targets of jihad included children and women. He didn't care about a person's sex or age. He believed in ridding the world of all non-Muslims.

## MILITANT ACTIVITY

Most of what is known about the life of Osama bin Laden has to do with his militant and criminal activities. With that being said, there are details of this aspect of his life that remain completely foreign to many.

Listed below are 24 things that may surprise you about the militant and criminal activities of bin Laden:

54. Bin Laden was angered by the Soviet Union's invasion of Afghanistan. As a result, after he graduated from university in 1979, he left his home country and went to Afghanistan to fight in the jihad.

55. When bin Laden decided that he was going to lend his support in the Soviet-Afghani war, he traveled with materials from his family's construction company, which he gave to Muslim guerrillas. The guerrillas used these materials to build roads, tunnels and shelters in the Afghan mountains.

56. Bin Laden founded al-Qaeda (the Base) in 1988. Al-Qaeda was formed as a way to recruit Muslims to fight in the jihad. It is believed that this organization is operating in about 65 countries, and has approximately 50,000 members. According to Terrorism Issues (about.com), Al Qaeda has no particular home base, but has "cells" and alliances in various countries. They tend to be perceived promoting corrupted forms of Islam. "Much has been said about Al Qaeda's wish to re-establish an Islamic caliphate, a transnational government of all Muslims concerned with affairs of state and religion. Such statements should be seen as a form of political nostalgia for a past that seems less corrupt than the present, rather than as a practical or achievable goal of the group."

57. After the war in Afghanistan ended in 1989, bin Laden returned to Saudi Arabia. Upon his return, he began

working in his family's construction company; however, that didn't last long.

58. When bin Laden returned to Saudi Arabia, the government took away his passport and banned him from traveling outside the kingdom. This was their way of attempting to prevent him from speaking out against countries such as America and England.

59. Bin Laden was always outspokenly critical of the Riyadh government during the time of the Gulf War. He predicted that if American soldiers went to the Saudi Peninsula, they would never leave at the end of the war. This prediction proved to be accurate.

60. Eventually, the Saudi government officially instructed bin Laden to not give public talks and to keep a low profile. This was due to the fact that he was speaking out against countries with which the Saudi government was seeking alliances.

61. Bin Laden had his brother (who was very close to the royal family because of the Saudi bin Laden Group) get his travel ban lifted by telling him that he had some business to take care of in Pakistan. Bin Laden left and never returned.

62. After leaving the Saudi kingdom, bin Laden never stayed in Pakistan. He believed that if the Pakistani Intelligence had caught him, they would have promptly turned him over to the Saudi government.

63. In 1991, bin Laden fled to Sudan and became one of the thousands of refugee Muslims who sought asylum there. This was during the time that the Sudanese government, along with Muslims from around the world, thought that Sudan could become the first country to be solely Islamic.

64. Sudan is where bin Laden was able to transform the al-Qaeda group into a terrorist network. It was while in Sudan

that bin Laden managed to recruit a majority of his followers.

65. Bin Laden had two sets of followers – those that were very close to him and were linked to him by a chain of command, and a much larger circle of followers who weren't directly linked to him, but felt obliged to carry out his general commands. He frequently advocated holy war to his followers, but privately did not advocate the same to his own family. For example, he advised a son to continue his religious studies in the Persian Gulf kingdom of Qatar (per capita, the richest country on earth).[18]

66. The first time the United States government became aware of Osama bin Laden was in 1991 or 1992. He was not yet seen as a major threat, as the crimes of which he was accused at that point in time were considered to be petty.

67. In 1994, the Saudi government officially stripped bin Laden of his citizenship, in

addition to freezing all assets that he still had in the country. Shortly after this, he became anti-Saudi.

68. Despite the fact that bin Laden invested a lot in Sudan, he was expelled from the country in 1996, forcing him to move to Afghanistan with his wives and children. This expulsion from Sudan was due to international pressure the Sudanese were under from other countries for hosting and protecting a terrorist.

69. On August 23, 1996, bin Laden declared a jihad against the United States Special Forces. From Afghanistan, he signed and issued a declaration entitled, *"Message from Osama bin Laden to his Muslim Brothers in the Whole World and Especially in the Arabian Peninsula: Declaration of Jihad Against the Americans Occupying the Land of the Two Hold Mosques; Expel the Heretics from the Arabian Peninsula."*

70. Bin Laden's very first interview with the Western media was with ABC's Peter

Bergen in 1997. After that, his communications with the Western media were very limited.

71. In November of 1998, the United States indicted bin Laden on 224 counts of murder for the Tanzanian and Kenyan embassy bombings. Due to the fact that the U.S. State Department was unable to arrest bin Laden, the case was thrown out of court.

72. Tripoli and Madrid also indicted bin Laden on terrorism charges. These charges against him were ultimately dropped as well, as they were unable to arrest him.

73. Also in 1998, it is believed that bin Laden's al-Qaeda network joined forces with the Egyptian Islamic Jihad that was led by Ayman al-Zawahiri. The joining of these two forces resulted in many mass-killings around the world.

74. Contrary to popular belief, bin Laden never had any official relations with the

Saudi royal family or government. All communications from him to them were done via his brothers, as they were the ones that were closely linked to the royal family via the Saudi bin Laden Group.

75. It is claimed that bin Laden had official relations with the CIA or other American Special Forces. These allegations are believed to be false, as bin Laden was supposed to have despised all things American. However, could there be any possibility that bin Laden was able to play along with the CIA long enough to be able to use what he learned and obtained from the CIA to aid the jihad against America? This was postulated by Michael Moran (MSNBC):

> NEW YORK, Aug. 24, 1998 — At the CIA, it happens often enough to have a code name: Blowback. Simply defined, this is the term that describes an agent, an operative or an operation that has turned on its creators. Osama bin Laden, our new public enemy

Number 1, is the personification of blowback. And the fact that he is viewed as a hero by millions in the Islamic world proves again the old adage: Reap what you sow.

Moran went on to concede some points: Yes, the West needed Josef Stalin to defeat Hitler. Yes, there were times during the Cold War when supporting one villain (Cambodia's Lon Nol, for instance) would have been better than the alternative (Pol Pot). So yes, there are times when any nation must hold its nose and shake hands with the devil for the long-term good of the planet. But just as surely, there are times when the United States, faced with such moral dilemmas, should have resisted the temptation to act. Arming a multi-national coalition of Islamic extremists in Afghanistan during the 1980s - well after the destruction of the Marine barracks in Beirut or the hijacking of TWA

Flight 847 - was one of those times.

76. Pakistani Intelligence highly respected bin Laden, and they were thought to have leaked plans against him. This belief stems from the fact that information about operations to capture bin Laden that involved the Pakistani Intelligence always seemed to reach him.

77. United States Special Forces uncovered documents revealing that bin Laden encouraged his subordinates to constantly plan new attacks against Americans, inclusive of planning the assassinations of General David Petraeus and President Barack Obama.

## CAPTURE ATTEMPTS & PRESUMED DEATHS

It is common knowledge that there were several attempts to capture Osama bin Laden, as well as several stories about his presumed death. Did you know, however, that it wasn't only the Americans that wanted to capture him? Did you know anything about the stories behind his presumed deaths?

Find out more from the nine facts listed below:

78. The first time bin Laden appeared on the FBI's Ten Most Wanted Fugitives' list was on June 7, 1999. He was the 456$^{th}$ person to be listed. He was charged with: "*Murder of U.S. Nationals Outside the United States; Conspiracy to Murder U.S. Nationals Outside the United States; Attack on a Federal Facility Resulting in Death.*"

79. Bin Laden later appeared on the FBI's Top 22 Most Wanted Terrorists' list on

October 10, 2001. The charges brought against him were the same as those on the FBI's Ten Most Wanted Fugitives' list.

80. Osama bin Laden is still the only fugitive to have appeared on both FBI's Most Wanted lists. Today, he is listed as deceased on both lists.

81. In 1997, the Pakistani Intelligence (under orders from the Saudi government) arranged an operation to kidnap bin Laden. Information about the operation was leaked to him and he managed to escape to Qandahar.

82. Another attempt was made to kidnap bin Laden in late 1997. This operation was arranged to be carried out by the American Special Forces. Again, information about the kidnap attempt was leaked to bin Laden. He, in turn, made it public. The Americans then cancelled the operation.

83. The Pakistan Observer, on December 25, 2001, published a front page story of the alleged death of the leader of al-Qaeda. According to the story, his death was supposedly caused by a "serious lung complication."

84. On January 18, 2002, former President of Pakistan, Pervez Musharraf, announced that bin Laden had died in Afghanistan, supposedly from kidney failure as a result of not having access to a dialysis machine.

85. In December of 2009, the U.S. government admitted that they were uncertain of bin Laden's whereabouts. They didn't know whether he was in Pakistan or Afghanistan.

86. Initially, the U.S. State Department offered a $25 million reward for information leading to the capture of bin Laden. The reward was increased to $50 million on July 14, 2007. Another $2 million was added via a program that was funded and developed by the Air

Transport Association and the Airline Pilots Association. When it was all said and done, though, the reward money was never paid out. As reported by Matthew Cole in May 2011, "No one will receive the $25 million reward for the capture of <u>Osama bin Laden</u>, say U.S. officials, because the raid that killed the al Qaeda leader in Pakistan on May 2 was the result of electronic intelligence, not human informants."[19]

## LIFE ON THE ABBOTTABAD COMPOUND

For years, the United States government had no idea exactly where Osama bin Laden was located. It wasn't until late 2010 that they received information that he was hiding out in Pakistan. The CIA was eventually able to identify Osama's courier, who led them to the compound in Abbottabad.

A CIA-led operation (Operation Neptune Spear) was carried out on May 2, 2011, and Osama bin Laden was killed by Navy SEALs from SEAL Team Six.

Following are nine facts about Osama's life on the Abbottabad compound about which you probably had no idea:

87. Bin Laden took many precautions in order to help maintain a low profile. Vending machines packed with Pepsi and Coke were found on bin Laden's compound. These machines allowed the children and adults alike to enjoy a cold

pop without having to go to the store to purchase one, at the risk of being identified.

88. Bin Laden banned his children from surfing the internet and watching television. They were also prohibited from playing outside. He didn't want them watching stories about him on the news, and he feared that they could be identified if they played outside.

89. To keep his children occupied, bin Laden allowed them to start their own vegetable gardens, and he would occasionally judge them and award prizes to the winners. Also, in order to eliminate any discriminating evidence of the family's presence, all garbage was burned on the compound on which Osama lived, rather than being put out for collection.

90. Bin Laden was surrounded by bodyguards, and was said to have moved around with extreme care. It was reported that his guards "had an agreed

code word that, when uttered, would signify that enemy forces were approaching and that they must martyr themselves.

"Once bin Laden had been forced to flee to the town of Abbottabad, the intense secrecy surrounding his movements would have been far more easily breached. His apparent hideout was, for instance, close to a cinema, a police station and a hospital for women and children. In the wilds of the tribal regions his operation might have gone largely unnoticed. But it appeared that working from here, apparently in a mansion with no external communications, where residents burned their rubbish, was too much: too many suspicions were aroused."[20]

91. When the Navy SEAL operatives raided bin Laden's Abbottabad compound in 2011, they found a "fairly extensive" pornography collection. However, exactly who owned this collection is unknown, as at least three sets of families lived on the compound.

92. In the raid on bin Laden's compound, a combination of storage devices, hard drives and computers was recovered. Most of these contained home videos that documented life around the compound. For example, some videos showed animals walking around the yard.

93. One video that was confiscated showed bin Laden looking at pictures of himself on a television screen, suggesting that he liked to watch himself.

94. Neither bin Laden nor anyone living in the Abbottabad compound paid property taxes. Additionally, he disregarded building regulations, as the third floor of the compound was illegally built. Even so, the Pakistani Intelligence claimed that it had no idea that bin Laden was living in Abbottabad.

95. In the event that bin Laden needed to quickly escape an attack, he had emergency phone numbers and money

stitched inside his clothing. When Navy SEAL Team Six found and killed bin Laden, sewn into his clothing were two telephone numbers and approximately 500 Euros.

## AFTER BIN LADEN'S DEATH

After news about the death of Osama bin Laden became public, there were many speculations and even more questions that citizens of the world wanted answered. Two years after his death there are still many unanswered questions.

You'll find five facts about his death that you probably didn't know listed below:

96. A DNA sample was first taken from Osama's dead body to verify his identity, and then he was buried at sea. In an email on May 2, 2011, Rear Admiral Charles Gaouette stated, *"Traditional procedures for Islamic burial was followed. The deceased's body was washed (ablution) then placed in a white sheet. The body was placed in a weighted bag. A military officer read prepared religious remarks, which were translated into Arabic by a native speaker. After the words were complete, the body was placed on a prepared flat*

*board, tipped up, whereupon the*
*deceased's body slid into the sea."*

97. Bin Laden didn't receive a land burial,
as United States officials didn't want his
followers to transform his burial site into
a shrine. Furthermore, information about
the exact location of his sea burial was
never released to the public.

98. After bin Laden's death, three of his
wives were thought to be terrorists.
Charges against them were eventually
dropped. Two of the wives, who were
Saudis, were allowed to remain in Saudi
Arabia, while the other wife (who was
Yemeni) was given the opportunity to go
back to Yemen.

99. Although Osama bin Laden died on May
2, 2011, the United States Justice
Department didn't officially drop the
charges against him until June 17, 2011.

100. The private museum of the CIA has on
display the AK-47 that was found next to
Osama bin Laden's body. It is not

known how exactly the CIA acquired this gun, and this display will never be shown to the public.

## CONCLUSION

Even though bin Laden and al-Qaeda were responsible for numerous crimes against the world, it was revealed after his death that many persons between the ages of 13 and 20 had no idea who he was. On the other hand, there are those individuals who think they are experts on this man's life.

Chances are that you knew some facts about Osama bin Laden's life. However, after reading through the 100 facts listed in this book, you have probably realized that you didn't actually know very much about this man.

You might have been aware that bin Laden was a very wealthy man, but did you know, prior to reading this book, just how he became so wealthy? You might have thought that all bin Laden did was plot against non-Muslims, but did you know that he was a caring family man and enjoyed reading, writing poetry and playing football?

People who come to prominence in the public eye, whether for positive or negative reasons, tend to be complicated individuals. There are multiple dimensions to the sum total of each person. A lifetime of experiences makes each of us who we are. It was the same for Osama bin Laden. Unfortunately for his victims, his destiny was to internalize fanatical religious beliefs to an extreme that caused him to terrorize and murder many innocent people. Although bin Laden was one of the world's most dangerous men, he started out as an innocent child just like all the rest of us. What happened in the mind and heart of young Osama bin Laden that turned him into such a heinous individual, hell-bent on committing murderous crimes against humanity? Once he crossed the line from religious believer to zealous mass murderer, he lost the right to freely enjoy life and had to be dealt with as the terrible criminal he had become. This, too, was bin Laden's destiny.

Did you know before reading this book that bin Laden was actually a Saudi and not an Afghani or Pakistani? Imagine how fanatical his beliefs had to be for him to walk away from his family roots and the citizenship of his birth. While he did not renounce his Saudi citizenship, he effectively left it behind when he departed from the kingdom under false pretenses and continued with activities that resulted in the Saudi government revoking his citizenship.

Most of the information about bin Laden's life surrounds his criminal and militant activities. Within this book, however, you have seen surprising information about his younger life before he was famous. You have also seen some of the little-known details about the horrendous path he chose later in life that made him infamous.

Facts about the life of the world's most notorious terrorist are limited and may differ depending on the source. In any case, today you can say that you now know an additional 100 things about the life of Osama bin Laden.

# SOURCES

1 http://www.nydailynews.com/new-york/1-wtc-spire-bringing-full-height-article-1.1340224#ixzz2hGTuTC5U

2

http://www.express.co.uk/news/showbiz/364897/The-woman-who-nailed-Osama-bin-Laden

3 http://www.findagrave.com/cgi-bin/fg.cgi?page=gr&GRid=69220235

4 http://www.biography.com/people/osama-bin-laden-37172

5

http://www.cnn.com/2013/08/30/world/osama-bin-laden-fast-facts/index.html

6 http://www.findagrave.com/cgi-bin/fg.cgi?page=gr&GRid=69220235

7

http://www.alarabiya.net/articles/2010/08/18/116996.html

8

http://www.pbs.org/wgbh/pages/frontline/shows/binladen/who/bio.html

9

http://www.encyclopedia.com/topic/Osama_bi
n_Laden.aspx

10

http://www.historycommons.org/entity.jsp?enti
ty=abdullah_azzam

11

http://marriage.about.com/od/infamous/p/Marri
ages-Of-Osama-Bin-Laden-Osama-Bin-
Ladens-Wives.htm

12

http://www.doctorzebra.com/prez/a_binladen.
htm

13

http://usatoday30.usatoday.com/news/sept11/
2001/10/07/bin-family.htm

14 http://www.cbsnews.com/8301-
503543_162-6013795-503543.html

15

http://www.fbi.gov/wanted/wanted_terrorists/u
sama-bin-laden

16 http://www.biography.com/people/osama-
bin-laden-37172

17

http://latimesblogs.latimes.com/jacketcopy/20
08/09/osama-bin-laden.htm

18

http://www.cnn.com/2012/04/30/opinion/berge
n-bin-laden-document-trove/index.html
[19] http://abcnews.go.com/Blotter/osama-bin-
laden-reward-paid/story?id=13633236

20

http://www.telegraph.co.uk/news/worldnews/a
sia/afghanistan/8487353/ Osama-bin-Laden-
how-he-evaded-capture-for-so-long.html

# ADDITIONAL SOURCES

Sorted By Fact Number

1. http://edition.cnn.com/2013/08/30/world/ osama-bin-laden-fast-facts/index.html

2. http://en.wikipedia.org/wiki/Osama_bin_La den and http://www.pbs.org/wgbh/pages/frontline/ shows/binladen/who/bio.html

3. http://edition.cnn.com/2013/08/30/world/ osama-bin-laden-fast-facts/index.html

4. http://books.google.com.jm/books?id=Pm_ 57NKwGwQC&pg=PT8&lpg=PT8&dq=osama +son+of+mohammed+son+of+awad+son+of +laden&source=bl&ots=ctU2ojFQwe&sig=w rhtB743G8xtUefUWrBUC3c_iPY&hl=en&sa= X&ei=34hXUp- FN5T64AP2h4GQBg&ved=0CGoQ6AEwCA#v =onepage&q=osama%20son%20of%20moh ammed%20son%20of%20awad%20son%20 of%20laden&f=false

5. http://en.wikipedia.org/wiki/Osama_bin_La den

6. http://gunh.com/5-facts-you-didnt-know-about-osama-bin-laden/

7. http://en.wikipedia.org/wiki/Osama_bin_La den

8. http://edition.cnn.com/2013/08/30/world/osama-bin-laden-fast-facts/index.html and http://en.wikipedia.org/wiki/Mohammed_b in_Awad_bin_Laden

9. http://en.wikipedia.org/wiki/Osama_bin_La den

10. http://www.pbs.org/wgbh/pages/frontline/shows/binladen/who/bio.html and http://edition.cnn.com/2013/08/30/world/osama-bin-laden-fast-facts/index.html

11. http://www.pbs.org/wgbh/pages/frontline/shows/binladen/who/bio.html and

http://en.wikipedia.org/wiki/Osama_bin_La
den

12. http://en.wikipedia.org/wiki/Mohammed_b
in_Awad_bin_Laden and
http://www.nndb.com/people/113/000055
945/

13. http://www.pbs.org/wgbh/pages/frontline/
shows/binladen/who/bio.html and
http://www.biography.com/people/osama-
bin-laden-37172

14. http://chcameron.tumblr.com/post/102055
43546/things-you-probably-didnt-know-
about-osama-bin-laden

15. http://chcameron.tumblr.com/post/102055
43546/things-you-probably-didnt-know-
about-osama-bin-laden

16. http://en.wikipedia.org/wiki/Osama_bin_La
den and
http://en.wikipedia.org/wiki/Wahhabi

17. http://www.pbs.org/wgbh/pages/frontline/shows/binladen/who/bio.html

18. http://en.wikipedia.org/wiki/Osama_bin_Laden

19. http://www.pbs.org/wgbh/pages/frontline/shows/binladen/who/bio.html and http://edition.cnn.com/2013/08/30/world/osama-bin-laden-fast-facts/index.html

20. http://edition.cnn.com/2013/08/30/world/osama-bin-laden-fast-facts/index.html

21. http://edition.cnn.com/2013/08/30/world/osama-bin-laden-fast-facts/index.html

22. http://chcameron.tumblr.com/post/10205543546/things-you-probably-didnt-know-about-osama-bin-laden and http://www.historycommons.org/timeline.jsp?other_al-qaeda_operatives=osamaBinLaden&timeline=complete_911_timeline

23. http://en.wikipedia.org/wiki/Bin_Laden_fa mily and http://www.pbs.org/wgbh/pages/frontline/ shows/binladen/who/bio2.html

24. http://en.wikipedia.org/wiki/Osama_bin_La den

25. http://edition.cnn.com/2013/08/30/world/ osama-bin-laden-fast-facts/index.html

26. http://www.pbs.org/wgbh/pages/frontline/ shows/binladen/who/bio2.html

27. http://www.pbs.org/wgbh/pages/frontline/ shows/binladen/who/bio.html

28. http://www.pbs.org/wgbh/pages/frontline/ shows/binladen/who/bio.html

29. http://www.pbs.org/wgbh/pages/frontline/ shows/binladen/who/bio2.html

30. http://www.pbs.org/wgbh/pages/frontline/ shows/binladen/who/bio2.html

31. http://www.pbs.org/wgbh/pages/frontline/ shows/binladen/who/bio2.html

32. http://www.fbi.gov/wanted/topten/usama-bin-laden

33. http://www.fbi.gov/wanted/topten/usama-bin-laden

34. http://latimesblogs.latimes.com/jacketcopy /2008/09/osama-bin-laden.html

35. http://en.wikipedia.org/wiki/Osama_bin_La den **and** http://martinslibrary.blogspot.com/2013/0 4/history-of-osama-bin-laden-life-and.html

36. http://www.huffingtonpost.com/2013/07/0 9/osama-bin-laden-report_n_3565861.html

37. http://www.cracked.com/quick-fixes/4-bizarre-low-budget-ways-osama-bin-laden-evaded-capture/

38. http://www.imdb.com/name/nm1136915/bio and http://www.pbs.org/wgbh/pages/frontline/shows/binladen/who/bio.html

39. http://en.wikipedia.org/wiki/Osama_bin_Laden and http://www.fbi.gov/wanted/topten/usama-bin-laden

40. http://www.pbs.org/wgbh/pages/frontline/shows/binladen/who/bio2.html

41. http://www.pbs.org/wgbh/pages/frontline/shows/binladen/who/bio2.html

42. http://www.cracked.com/quick-fixes/4-bizarre-low-budget-ways-osama-bin-laden-evaded-capture/

43. http://www.cracked.com/quick-fixes/4-bizarre-low-budget-ways-osama-bin-laden-evaded-capture/

44. http://www.imdb.com/name/nm1136915/
bio and
http://en.wikipedia.org/wiki/Les_Guignols_
de_l'info

45. http://www.pbs.org/wgbh/pages/frontline/
shows/binladen/who/bio2.html

46. http://www.pbs.org/wgbh/pages/frontline/
shows/binladen/who/bio.html

47. http://chcameron.tumblr.com/post/102055
43546/things-you-probably-didnt-know-
about-osama-bin-laden

48. http://www.pbs.org/wgbh/pages/frontline/
shows/binladen/who/bio2.html

49. http://www.pbs.org/wgbh/pages/frontline/
shows/binladen/who/bio2.html

50. http://www.pbs.org/wgbh/pages/frontline/
shows/binladen/who/bio2.html

51. http://www.pbs.org/wgbh/pages/frontline/ shows/binladen/who/bio2.html and http://en.wikipedia.org/wiki/Osama_bin_La den

52. http://en.wikipedia.org/wiki/Osama_bin_La den and http://edition.cnn.com/2013/08/30/world/ osama-bin-laden-fast-facts/index.html

53. http://en.wikipedia.org/wiki/Osama_bin_La den

54. http://www.pbs.org/wgbh/pages/frontline/ shows/binladen/who/bio.html and http://edition.cnn.com/2013/08/30/world/ osama-bin-laden-fast-facts/index.html

55. http://www.pbs.org/wgbh/pages/frontline/ shows/binladen/who/bio.html and http://edition.cnn.com/2013/08/30/world/ osama-bin-laden-fast-facts/index.html

56. http://www.pbs.org/wgbh/pages/frontline/ shows/binladen/who/bio.html and

http://edition.cnn.com/2013/08/30/world/
osama-bin-laden-fast-facts/index.html and
http://www.start.umd.edu/start/data_colle
ctions/tops/terrorist_organization_profile.a
sp?id=6

57. http://edition.cnn.com/2013/08/30/world/
osama-bin-laden-fast-facts/index.html

58. http://www.pbs.org/wgbh/pages/frontline/
shows/binladen/who/bio.html

59. http://www.biography.com/people/osama-
bin-laden-37172 (the video)

60. http://www.pbs.org/wgbh/pages/frontline/
shows/binladen/who/bio.html

61. http://www.pbs.org/wgbh/pages/frontline/
shows/binladen/who/bio.html

62. http://www.pbs.org/wgbh/pages/frontline/
shows/binladen/who/bio.html

63. http://www.pbs.org/wgbh/pages/frontline/ shows/binladen/who/bio.html and http://www.biography.com/people/osama-bin-laden-37172 (the video)

64. http://www.biography.com/people/osama-bin-laden-37172 (the video)

65. http://www.pbs.org/wgbh/pages/frontline/ shows/binladen/who/bio2.html

66. http://www.biography.com/people/osama-bin-laden-37172 (the video)

67. http://edition.cnn.com/2013/08/30/world/ osama-bin-laden-fast-facts/index.html and http://www.pbs.org/wgbh/pages/frontline/ shows/binladen/who/bio.html

68. http://www.pbs.org/wgbh/pages/frontline/ shows/binladen/who/bio.html and http://edition.cnn.com/2013/08/30/world/ osama-bin-laden-fast-facts/index.html

69. http://edition.cnn.com/2013/08/30/world/ osama-bin-laden-fast-facts/index.html

70. http://edition.cnn.com/2013/08/30/world/ osama-bin-laden-fast-facts/index.html

71. http://edition.cnn.com/2013/08/30/world/ osama-bin-laden-fast-facts/index.html

72. http://en.wikipedia.org/wiki/Osama_bin_La den

73. http://edition.cnn.com/2013/08/30/world/ osama-bin-laden-fast-facts/index.html

74. http://www.pbs.org/wgbh/pages/frontline/ shows/binladen/who/bio2.html

75. http://www.pbs.org/wgbh/pages/frontline/ shows/binladen/who/bio2.html

76. http://www.pbs.org/wgbh/pages/frontline/ shows/binladen/who/bio2.html

77. http://abcnews.go.com/Blotter/osama-bin-laden-letters-al-qaeda-leader-frustrated/story?id=16268578

78. http://edition.cnn.com/2013/08/30/world/osama-bin-laden-fast-facts/index.html and http://www.fbi.gov/wanted/topten/usama-bin-laden

79. http://www.historycommons.org/context.jsp?item=a101001FBIList22 and http://www.fbi.gov/wanted/wanted_terrorists/usama-bin-laden

80. http://en.wikipedia.org/wiki/Osama_bin_Laden and http://www.fbi.gov/wanted/wanted_terrorists/usama-bin-laden and http://www.fbi.gov/wanted/topten/usama-bin-laden

81. http://en.wikipedia.org/wiki/Osama_bin_Laden

82. http://www.pbs.org/wgbh/pages/frontline/shows/binladen/who/bio2.html

83. http://www.pbs.org/wgbh/pages/frontline/shows/binladen/who/bio2.html

84. http://edition.cnn.com/2013/08/30/world/osama-bin-laden-fast-facts/index.html

85. http://edition.cnn.com/2013/08/30/world/osama-bin-laden-fast-facts/index.html

86. http://edition.cnn.com/2013/08/30/world/osama-bin-laden-fast-facts/index.html

87. http://www.huffingtonpost.co.uk/2012/04/30/osama-bin-laden-10-things-we-found-out_n_1464942.html

88. http://www.huffingtonpost.co.uk/2012/04/30/osama-bin-laden-10-things-we-found-out_n_1464942.html

89. http://www.cracked.com/quick-fixes/4-bizarre-low-budget-ways-osama-bin-laden-evaded-capture/

90. http://www.cracked.com/quick-fixes/4-bizarre-low-budget-ways-osama-bin-laden-evaded-capture/

91. http://www.reuters.com/article/2011/05/13/us-binladen-porn-idUSTRE74C4RK20110513

92. http://abcnews.go.com/Blotter/osama-bin-laden-home-videos-released-compound-raid/story?id=13555615

93. http://abcnews.go.com/Blotter/osama-bin-laden-home-videos-released-compound-raid/story?id=13555615

94. http://www.theguardian.com/world/2013/jul/09/abbottabad-report-osama-bin-laden

95. http://www.huffingtonpost.co.uk/2012/04/
30/osama-bin-laden-10-things-we-found-
out_n_1464942.html

96. http://www.businessinsider.com/details-of-
osama-bin-ladens-secret-burial-at-sea-
revealed-in-military-emails-2012-11

97. http://www.theguardian.com/world/2011/
may/02/sea-burial-osama-bin-laden

98. http://www.huffingtonpost.co.uk/2012/04/
30/osama-bin-laden-10-things-we-found-
out_n_1464942.html

99. http://edition.cnn.com/2013/08/30/world/
osama-bin-laden-fast-facts/index.html

100.    http://www.complex.com/art-
design/2013/07/cia-museum-bin-laden-gun

www.ingramcontent.com/pod-product-compliance
Lightning Source LLC
Chambersburg PA
CBHW071423040426
42445CB00012BA/1278